GLORIA FURMAN

MISSIONAL MOTHERHOOD

THE BIBLE STUDY

THE EVERYDAY MINISTRY OF MOTHERHOOD
IN THE GRAND PLAN OF GOD

TGC THE GOSPEL **COALITION**
WOMEN'S INITIATIVES

LifeWay Press®
Nashville, Tennessee

ISBN: 9781430054405
Item: 006101512

Dewey Decimal Classification: 306.874
Subject Headings: MOTHERS \ MOTHER AND CHILD \ WOMEN

All Scripture quotations, unless otherwise noted, are taken from The Holy Bible, English Standard Version® (ESV®), copyright © 2001 by Crossway, a publishing ministry of Good News Publishers. Used by permission. All rights reserved. Scripture quotations marked NIV are taken from The Holy Bible, NEW INTERNATIONAL VERSION®, Copyright © 1973, 1978, 1984, 2011 by Biblica, Inc. All rights reserved worldwide. Used by permission. Scripture quotations marked NASB is taken from the New American Standard Bible®, Copyright © 1960, 1962, 1963, 1968, 1971, 1972, 1973, 1975, 1977, 1995 by The Lockman Foundation. Used by permission. (www.lockman.org)

To order additional copies of this resource, order online at www.lifeway.com; write LifeWay Christian Resources Customer Service: One LifeWay Plaza, Nashville, TN 37234-0113; fax order to 615.251.5933; or call toll-free 1.800.458.2772.
Printed in the United States of America

Adult Ministry Publishing
LifeWay Resources
One LifeWay Plaza
Nashville, TN 37234-0152

PRODUCTION TEAM

Author:
Gloria Furman

Content Editor:
Mike Wakefield

Editorial Project Leader:
Michelle Hicks

Editorial Manager:
Amy Lowe

Production Editor:
Elizabeth Hyndman

Video Producer &
Director:
Rick Simms

Art Director:
Heather Wetherington

Director, LifeWay
Adult Ministry:
Faith Whatley

CONTENTS

ABOUT THE AUTHOR

 Gloria Furman is a wife, mother of four, cross-cultural worker, and writer. In 2008, her family moved to the Middle East to plant Redeemer Church of Dubai where her husband, Dave, serves as the pastor. She is the author of *Glimpses of Grace, Treasuring Christ When Your Hands Are Full*, *The Pastor's Wife*, and *Missional Motherhood*.

A NOTE FROM GLORIA

Hello!

Greetings from the sandy Arabian Peninsula. As the sun rose this morning over our city, I was reminded of what it says in God's Word—His mercies are new every morning (Lam. 3:22-23). Taking in the brilliant desert sunrise usually makes me think of my friends and family in different parts of the world going about their days or nights. It makes me smile to remember that it's always morning somewhere. God's mercy to us in Christ is ever present, day or night.

I'm thinking of you and praying for you as you take part in this study wherever you may be—from the bustling mega-cities in India to the picturesque fields in rural Indiana. We serve a great God—the only God—and I'm eager to talk about Him with you and discuss His plan to glorify Himself through the strategic, missional ministry of motherhood.

In Christ,

Gloria

HOW TO USE THIS STUDY

Welcome to *Missional Motherhood!* This six-session Bible study can be used in a number of settings. It's primarily designed to be used in a weekly small group setting with a leader and a small gathering of women. However, the study can also be used as an individual study, in a one-on-one mentoring relationship, or with a large group of women. Because this study is only six sessions, it's also possible to use this in a retreat setting. If used in this way, you will need to carve out time and perhaps find creative ways for participants to complete the personal study between group meetings.

STUDY ELEMENTS

GROUP SESSION

During the Group Session you will discuss and process together what you are learning through the video teaching and the personal study. Each Group Session will consist of three parts:

REVIEW: A list of questions will help you assess and discuss what you've studied in your personal study time.

WATCH: Following the review, you'll watch the video teaching for the session. Space is provided for you to take notes on the teaching.

DISCUSS: Review and process the video teaching as a group, using the questions provided.

CLOSE: A suggested final prayer prompt or activity closes the Group Session.

PERSONAL STUDY

There are four Personal Study sections each week. This material will give you an opportunity to dig deeper into some of the themes discussed in the video and help you preview what's coming in the next session. You can complete all of these at one setting. However, it would probably be best to space the personal study activities out through the week to give you time to ponder the truth and how to apply it.

NOTE TO GROUP LEADER

The Group Session portion of Session 1 is different from the other group sessions. It contains more information, providing an introduction to the study, and lays a foundation for what will take place in the weeks to follow. As the leader, you will need to handle this material differently from the other Group Sessions. You may choose to present it by sharing the information in your own words, sprinkling in some of the discussion questions provided. A second option would be to divide the material among your participants, allowing groups of 2-4 women to discuss specific sections then present their sections of material to the larger group. Or you may choose to treat it as a personal study time, allowing participants to read and respond to the questions individually, then discussing the material in a large group setting.

"It's true for me, if I believe it"

are standards of right + wrong mere products of time + culture?

ABOUT THE GOSPEL COALITION

Denies moral truth from Bible

The Gospel Coalition is a fellowship of evangelical churches deeply committed to renewing our faith in the gospel of Christ and to reforming our ministry practices to conform fully to the Scriptures. We have become deeply concerned about some movements within traditional evangelicalism that seem to be diminishing the church's life and leading us away from our historic beliefs and practices. On the one hand, we are troubled by the idolatry of personal consumerism and the politicization of faith; on the other hand, we are distressed by the unchallenged acceptance of theological and moral relativism. These movements have led to the easy abandonment of both biblical truth and the transformed living mandated by our historic faith. We not only hear of these influences, we see their effects. We have committed ourselves to invigorating churches with new hope and compelling joy based on the promises received by grace alone through faith alone in Christ alone.

We believe that in many evangelical churches a deep and broad consensus exists regarding the truths of the gospel. Yet we often see the celebration of our union with Christ replaced by the age-old attractions of power and affluence, or by monastic retreats into ritual, liturgy, and sacrament. What replaces the gospel will never promote a mission-hearted faith anchored in enduring truth working itself out in unashamed discipleship eager to stand the tests of kingdom-calling and sacrifice. We desire to advance along the King's highway, always aiming to provide gospel advocacy, encouragement, and education so that current and next-generation church leaders are better equipped to fuel their ministries with principles and practices that glorify the Savior and do good to those for whom He shed His life's blood.

We want to generate a unified effort among all peoples—an effort that is zealous to honor Christ and multiply His disciples, joining in a true coalition for Jesus. Such a biblically grounded and united mission is the only enduring future for the church. This reality compels us to stand with others who are stirred by the conviction that the mercy of God in Jesus Christ is our only hope of eternal salvation. We desire to champion this gospel with clarity, compassion, courage, and joy—gladly linking hearts with fellow believers across denominational, ethnic, and class lines.

Our desire is to serve the church we love by inviting all our brothers and sisters to join us in an effort to renew the contemporary church in the ancient gospel of Christ so we truly speak and live for Him in a way that clearly communicates to our age. As pastors, we intend to do this in our churches through the ordinary means of His grace: prayer, ministry of the Word, baptism and the Lord's Supper, and the fellowship of the saints. We yearn to work with all who seek the lordship of Christ over the whole of life with unabashed hope in the power of the Holy Spirit to transform individuals, communities, and cultures.

SESSION 1:

INTRODUCTION

Welcome to *Missional Motherhood*! My hope is that God would use this study to strengthen your faith as you go about your everyday ministry of motherhood. I truly believe that when we take a step back and understand what the Bible says about the grand plan of God, then the details in life (like motherhood) come into clearer focus.

Before we dive into the introduction of this study, let's take a few minutes to introduce ourselves to one another:

Share your name and a little information about your family and your neighborhood.

Share what drew you to this study.

With just a tap of my finger, I can make the camera lens on my phone zoom in to take a close-up photo. If I want to take in more of the big picture, though, I have to take a few steps back. Some Bible studies are like the zoom feature, helping you focus very closely on one specific passage of Scripture. However, this study will ask you to step back and take in the panorama of life as we read about it in the Bible. There is something of value in taking steps back on a regular basis to see and remember the grand plan of God. This exercise is especially helpful as we seek to nurture life. Knowing the big picture helps us appreciate the thousands of little details of our work as mothering women.

Our pace for this study will be quick, but our discoveries will leave an impact on our lives for a long time. We are taking a wide-angle look at God's grand plan, but don't disable your zoom feature quite yet. We're going to need a close-up look at the Scripture in order to apply God's Word to our motherhood.

Have you ever told a temper-tantruming toddler to "use their words"? Me too. When we talk about theology and motherhood, we not only need to "use our words," we need to use the right words. We need to be intentional when we "use our words," especially words about who God is and what He is doing. But we also need to be intentional with our words about motherhood. So, let's talk about some of the words that are going to keep coming up in our discussions:

In your own words, briefly describe "God's grand plan."

What comes to your mind when you think of "missional"?

What comes to your mind when you think of "motherhood"?

One time I took my children to visit a farm that had a barn loft filled with incubators. Being desert-dwellers their entire lives, my kids had never been to a farm before. In the loft hundreds of chicken eggs were being warmed in neat little rows and cages lined the walls for the tiny birds who had already hatched. As we *ooh*-ed and *aah*-ed at the rows of eggs and the cheeping masses of fluffy chicks, one of my kids expressed alarm at the fact that there were no grown chickens in the loft. "Oh no! Where are their mommies?"

Perhaps you've heard the expression that someone is a "mother hen." The image that comes to mind is of a female chicken, her wings spread out to envelop a bunch of baby chicks. We might call a girl or woman a "mother hen" because of the attention and care she gives to others. She receives this nickname because of what she does, versus her biological connection to the people she nurtures. I share this illustration not to make you think of feathers and omelets, but to point out the fact that "mother" is a verb, too.

Mothering (or nurturing) is a calling for every woman, including those who do not have biological or adopted children. There is so much that falls under the umbrella of our mothering, nurturing work: caregiving, showing hospitality, discipling, teaching, raising children, serving, and more. Every Christian woman is called to the spiritual motherhood of making disciples of all nations.

Each of us comes from various life circumstances. No two women, no two families, no two churches, and no two neighborhoods are the same. What are some of the "and more" things that fall under the umbrella of the mothering, nurturing work that you do?

Who are the women in your life who have nurtured your faith in God, "spiritually mothering" you? What makes them unique? What do they have in common?

Over the next six weeks we are going to explore the idea that the everyday ministry of motherhood is, by nature, missional. It is missional because God created motherhood for His purpose—to glorify Himself.

READ EPHESIANS 2:8-10. What words stand out to you?

What does this text say about the nature of our salvation in Christ?

What does this text say about the nature of the good works that we do?

Salvation by grace alone through faith alone is a foundational doctrine of Christianity. Without it, Christianity is a mere religious system that has no power to truly save. While many of us know this doctrine, we are still tempted at times to add on our works to justify ourselves or to use as bargaining chips when pleading with God for our children's salvation.

Do you feel like the truths of Ephesians 2:8-10 reflect your beliefs and experiences of the Christian faith? Why or why not?

In the coming sessions we will repeatedly come back to the thesis of missional motherhood:

Jesus invites women to missional motherhood: to follow His pattern, to trust His promises, and to nurture others by the power He provides.

Well, we have a lot to talk about! I'm eager to step back with you and take in the big picture, then dig into some specific texts to discover what they mean for our motherhood. Before we go any further, take a few moments to pray together and ask God to open your eyes, so that we might behold wonderful things in His Word (Ps. 119:18).

WATCH

Use the space below to take notes on the Session 1 video.

DISCUSS

How would you define missional motherhood in your own words?

Have you ever fallen into that "I'm just a mom" trap? Explain. How does that way of thinking hinder your ability to see the big picture of what God wants to do through you?

How does understanding motherhood as a calling change the way you approach it?

What is tyranny of the urgent and how does it affect your motherhood?

What are some of those urgent things that get in the way of doing what's most important?

What do you most want to get out of this Bible study? Why?

CLOSE

Break into small groups and spend time praying for each other. Ask God to give you new eyes to see yourselves as God sees you and a willingness to take up the challenge of being a missional mom.

ONE

Welcome to your personal study time! In the group session, we talked about how our focus on the details of life is renewed when we take a step back to survey the big picture of God's story. This 10,000-foot view of life is so helpful, especially when we're puzzled, indifferent, or even frustrated by the situations we see unfolding in our daily lives.

Specifically, we're zooming in on the topic of motherhood in this study, but in order to do that we are zooming out to see God's grand plan. We're reading in Scripture how God uses motherhood to bring Himself glory. After all, that is the goal of motherhood—to glorify God.

> *From culture to culture, there are different views concerning the goal of motherhood. How does your particular culture view the goal of motherhood? How does this view differ from other cultures?*

If you're new to the Christian faith, words like *glory* and *glorify* can feel like heavy lifting for your mind to consider. If that's you, then I want to encourage you; your feelings are right in line with reality! The word *glory* in the Bible comes from a root word—a verb—that means *to be heavy, weighty, or burdensome.* Glory carries the connotation of heavy abundance and weighty honor. Glory is substantive and real, not flimsy and imaginary. To glorify God is to ascribe to God the abundant, weighty honor that He is due. It is to acknowledge God as glorious as He really is. When we glorify God we are not adding to Him as though we could make Him complete; we are humble creatures adoring His manifold perfections.

God's glory necessarily elicits a response from us. Let's dig a little deeper into this idea by looking at a "missions song" that was composed in response to God's glory.

READ PSALM 96. Look up the word *ascribe* in the dictionary and write the definitions.

ascribe → assign

Psalm 96 is a globally-resonating "missions song."
READ ALL THE WAY THROUGH PSALM 96 THREE TIMES. Next, mark the places where you see the words *glory* and *ascribe.*

Make a list of all the reasons the psalmist gives for why the people (and all the earth) should ascribe glory to the Lord.

READ THROUGH PSALM 96 THREE MORE TIMES. Now mark all of the places where you see verbal command words like *say, declare, tell, and* sing.

According to Psalm 96, what is the appropriate response to God's glory?

Who is being called to respond to God's glory in these ways?

Sometimes it is difficult for us to see how our everyday ministry of motherhood can have any influence in missions—God's global "call to worship." Have you ever struggled with this? Explain.

In your reflections from our group session, and especially in light of Psalm 96, what connections can you see between God's grand plan to glorify Himself in all the nations and your motherhood?

TWO

In our area of the world, the weather is fairly predictable for the vast majority of the year. I rarely (if ever) open the weather app on my phone. We just know it's going to be hot and dusty. The only question is how hot. Every once in a while, a northwest *shamal* or a southern wind from the Saudi Arabian "Empty Quarter" will blow across the country, kicking up a sandstorm. During these sandstorms we have to make sure the windows are closed; otherwise everything will get covered in a gritty layer of sand. The clouds of sand can even cover up the sun. This sun-covering effect is disorienting (and even a bit creepy).

Losing sight of God's glory is similar to the sandstorms. As we go about our everyday lives—raising our children, discipling young women, working, and serving others—we tend to assume our priorities will remain intact. But assuming leads to forgetting. As the sandstorm of our everyday lives swirls about us, we forget the orienting, illuminating purpose for our lives: to glorify God. We can become disoriented, losing sight of what's most important. After all, the glory of God is what we live for.

The following verses tell us how glorifying God should be at the center of all we do. Write out the verses below in your own words.

Colossians 3:17

1 Corinthians 10:31

1 Peter 4:11

It is evident from these verses and the rest of Scripture that we should glorify God in all we do. In our everyday, in our mothering and nurturing, we should seek to glorify Him.

By virtue of our salvation in Christ and identification with Him in His death and resurrection, every single Christian ought to have a missionary heartbeat. Homemakers, students, widows, children, and businesswomen—all of us are given the exciting privilege of ascribing glory to God among the nations wherever God has placed us. The gospel message and our privilege of sharing it are worth singing about! God has a global plan for His glory, and it is our joy to participate in giving Him the glory He is due with our hearts, deeds, eating/drinking, speaking, serving, and whatever we do.

That "whatever we do" is different for all of us. My mind is just swimming with all of the various ways the women I know are bringing glory to God! Amy* feels like she is 38,000 weeks pregnant, and she is praising God for persevering her body. Lena* is struggling with her family's transition to a new country, and she is telling the Lord (and her daughters) how she needs God's help every hour. Hyejin* is shepherding her son through difficulties in his school and telling him to ask God for wisdom. Kalla* works hard from sunup to sundown, and she talks with the people she sits next to on the bus and her coworkers about her Savior.

What are some of the ways that you glorify God through your ministry to the individuals in your life?

moms → nurturing * with love & prayer

* Names have been changed.

THREE

The Session 1 video introduced you to the idea that the nature of our everyday ministry of motherhood is missional. Mothering work is missional because God created us, and He ordained every single one of our ministries to bring glory to Himself. God has incorporated us into His global mission—so our missional influence expands from our baby's crib to our desks at the office to our next door neighbors and to our neighbors among the nations.

I can issue a dozen "mission statements" like this a day: "Guys, we need to get ready on time this morning." "I'm going to get this to-do list done." "So-and-so is coming over, and we're going to read Colossians together." "We're having Mexican food for dinner!" (That last one was probably more of a victory cry than a mission statement.) However, of all the mission statements that pass through our minds as we go about our daily lives, there is one all-encompassing, exhilarating mission that preoccupies our thoughts. It is what Jesus said to His disciples just before He ascended back into heaven to be enthroned at God's right hand:

> And Jesus came and said to them, "All authority in heaven and on earth has been given to me. Go therefore and make disciples of all nations, baptizing them in the name of the Father and of the Son and of the Holy Spirit, teaching them to observe all that I have commanded you. And behold, I am with you always, to the end of the age."
>
> MATTHEW 28:18-20

We're going to spend time discussing the "Great Commission" in future sessions, but for now, let's talk about first and previous impressions.

What are your first impressions of this passage?

List any previous impressions you may have had.

What are some of the commonly held beliefs/attitudes about the work of nurturing others? How about discipling younger women? Raising and discipling children? Evangelizing your neighbors?

Does Matthew 28:18-20 come into conflict with any commonly held beliefs or attitudes about the work of mothering/nurturing others? In what way?

I hope this text helps clarify for you the focus of this study on missional motherhood. The priority of our ministry on this side of eternity is helping prepare others for eternity, too, by evangelizing and discipling the nations.

Based on what you've read, heard, and discussed so far, where do you think motherhood fits into this big picture?

My prayer for you is that you would be thrilled to see the significant meaning of your motherhood in the grand plan of God. The One who created all things is worthy to receive glory and honor and power (Rev. 4:11). God did not create you to be "just" a mom. By His will you were created for His glory. Those are profound and encouraging thoughts.

FOUR

I don't know all the circumstances you will be confronted with today. It would be silly for me to try and address all of the issues that women are facing across the world. But there is one Book that does speak to our greatest obstacles, our most daunting hindrances, and our most desperate situations: the Bible.

The Bible tells us who God is and how we can know Him. It points out that our most important need is for a right relationship with God. Every other need you have pales in comparison, like an ant hiding in his dust-bunny house in the basement of a Shanghai skyscraper.

Now, if there was ever a controversial statement to make then it was that one! Even at this very moment, I feel like the biggest need I have is for a more effective decongestant for this nagging sinus pain. And something convenient to eat for lunch. And …

What about you? What feels like the most urgent need you have right now?

Every other need you experience points you to the one great need of knowing and being known by God. Are you hungry? Hunger is a pointer to help you see that you were designed to live by every word that proceeds from the mouth of God. Are you thirsty? Thirst is a pointer to help you see that your spiritual thirst can only be quenched by the living water Jesus gives. Are you cold? Afraid? Restless? Sad? Lonely? Lost? These needs point you to the one and only God who made you, loves you, and gave His Son to die in your place so you could love Him back in spirit and truth forever.

Do you feel eternity beating in your heart?

How does your answer to the previous question point you to your need for God?

These pictures and pointers serve to remind us of eternal truth. And we need all the reminders we can get! It is astounding to consider all of the contrary messages (i.e., lies) we are faced with each day. According to the world, life is generally meaningless and humanity is only a group of optimistic clumps of cells. So, a growling stomach simply exists to remind you that you skipped lunch and nothing more. But the Bible renews our minds, so that we can see through the lies of this world. This clarity is critical for missional motherhood. What woman hasn't been lied to about who God is, why He made the world, and what motherhood means? The course of this world would have us live as zombies— dead to God and our desperate need for Him.

What are some of the lies about God that your culture tells mothers and women specifically?

We're going to talk about this passage in a few weeks, but for now let's work on committing Romans 12:1-2 to memory. In lieu of answering more questions today, spend some time meditating on that passage.

Praise God that He has not left us to our own devices to plod along like zombies, simply following the course of this world without interruption. He has intervened. He has revealed Himself in His Word and sent His Son, the Word made flesh. In God's Word, the Bible, we read the real story. There's so much more we can say about this, but for now, let's look forward to gathering together to hear and discuss this real story.

MOTHERHOOD IN THE GRAND PLAN OF GOD: NURTURING LIFE IN THE FACE OF DEATH

REVIEW

Welcome to Session 2 of *Missional Motherhood*! Let's begin by reviewing your personal study from last week.

What would you say is the goal of motherhood?

How would you define God's glory?

What is the connection between God's plan to glorify Himself and your motherhood?

How do you glorify God through your ministry to others each day?

What "mission statements" do you make each day?

How does Jesus' mission statement (Matt. 28:19-20) affect how you mother or nurture others?

How is motherhood a part of the priority of reaching the nations for Christ?

WATCH

Use the space below to take notes on the Session 2 video.

MISSIONAL MOTHERHOOD

DISCUSS

Use the following questions to debrief the teaching from the Session 2 video.

Does God's big story make sense to you? Explain.

How do we see God's plan to redeem humankind from the beginning of Scripture?

Why is seeing God's big picture so important to missional motherhood?

How do you see God's heart to rescue and redeem humankind throughout the Old Testament?

How did the death, burial, and resurrection of Christ change everything?

CLOSE

Lead each person in your group to choose a partner. Direct the group members to share with their partners the name of someone who needs to better understand God's big story. Take time to pray specifically for each person.

ONE

Have you ever looked at a verse from the Bible and thought to yourself, *Ha! There's no way I can do that!* Here's one that I've wrestled with over the years:

> *Set your minds on things that are above, not on things that are on earth.*

COLOSSIANS 3:2

At first glance, this one verse seems utterly out of touch with those of us who have to, you know, pay attention to things on earth, like chasing curious toddlers, returning phone calls, adjusting quarterly budgets, watching the pot on the stove, and shifting lanes while driving. How are we supposed to set our minds on things that are above when the things on the earth are so urgent and necessary?

Well, if we only take one Bible verse at a time and give each verse just a cursory glance, we won't arrive at any conclusions that the Author intended. To best understand the meaning of a passage of Scripture, we must understand its context.

The context for Colossians 3:2 is the rest of the argument, the rest of the letter, the rest of the New Testament, and the rest of the Bible. In other words, because this verse is in the Bible, it is not utterly out of touch, but rather, it is able to make us wise for salvation, is God-breathed, and is profitable for teaching, for reproof, for correction, and for training in righteousness. All this is so that we may be complete, equipped for every good work (2 Tim. 3:15-17). Colossians 3:2 is there for the good of our souls.

So let's expand the context of that verse a bit. There's a whole grand story behind Paul's exhortation in Colossians 3:2, and we need to know that story in order to interpret the passage properly.

In the Session 2 video, I shared with you a super-speedy Bible overview. I had several goals in doing that, one being to help establish and/or remind us of the big picture of Scripture. When Paul wrote his Letter to the Colossians (and his other letters, too!) he often reminded his readers of the big picture. In fact, if you look for it, you'll notice the biblical writers established context in different ways—through listing genealogies, mentioning their historical time period, or referring to things past or "things to come."

The first few sentences in Colossians 3 are a brilliant example of this big picture reminder.

> *If then you have been raised with Christ, seek the things that are above, where Christ is, seated at the right hand of God.* **Past**
> *Set your minds on things that are above, not on things that are on earth. For you have died, and your life is hidden with Christ in God. When Christ who is your life appears, then you also will appear with Him in glory.*
>
> **COLOSSIANS 3:1-4**

In Colossians 3:1-4, what is Paul saying about:
The past?

The present?

The future?

It's so refreshing to step back to see the bigger picture, isn't it? It makes exhortations like "Set your minds on things that are above, not on things that are on earth" resound with joy-filled simplicity and reliable sensibility. Since we have died and risen with Christ, our lives are hidden with Him, and He's coming back for us, then of course we want to (and ought to) fill our minds with thoughts of Him! Even in the midst of our urgent, earth-based tasks, our minds can be preoccupied with Jesus—the beauty of His character, the astonishing mercy of what He's done for us, His patient work in the world today, and the mind-boggling reality of what He has promised to do in the future.

There are no more sweeter thoughts to entertain as we go about our everyday ministry of motherhood than thoughts of Jesus and the reality that is now in play because of Him.

What are some of the urgent, earth-based tasks that tend to overwhelm your thoughts?

How does this Scripture passage refresh your perspective on those tasks?

How would you communicate this refreshed perspective to another woman who has asked you, "How do you do what you do?"

Can you think of other Scripture passages that you would like to study further, specifically investigating them in light of their larger context? Who is someone you could study with?

The reality that is now in play because of Christ is the permanent, irreversible reality in which we live. And that is a mightily encouraging thought.

How will thoughts of the faithfulness of Jesus and the exciting prospect of His future grace change the way you see the rest of your day today?

Can you think of one or two other ladies in your life who could use the same encouragement? Write them a note or give them a call.

TWO

I think we mothers and spiritual mothers tend to feel like we are pretty central. I'm not saying that as a put-down, but as an observation of my own life and the lives of the women I know. When I say that we feel central, part of the reason is that sometimes we are, literally, central. Think of a swirling group of kindergarteners who flock to their teacher when the bell rings. Think of the young ladies who watch the doors of your church building, scanning the crowd for "her" to arrive—the older mother hen who mothers the single women. Think of the weary new moms who gravitate toward the older moms with questions, concerns, and prayer requests.

My point is this: the people in our lives know where to go for food, protection, and help. They know where to go to grow. They come to you, mothering woman, for provision. No pressure, right? Thankfully, we know that God is the One who is faithful to provide what they need. As nurturers in the middle of all these needs, we get to be the conduits of God's grace. That's what He designed us to be. So, of course, mothering women tend to feel "central."

My hope in reminding us of the big story is that we would see we are not the center of it. God is. I've prayed that you and the women you are gathering with would feel appropriately small, dependent, de-centralized, and yet, in a God-centered way, significant. God created motherhood for His glory, and that's something worth giving your life away for—a thousand moments a day in all those tiny ways, or in one final moment.

As we talked about earlier, the God who existed before time did not create anything meaningless. Women nurturing life in the face of death couldn't possibly be "just" moms. As Christ becomes the center of your life, God's pattern is played out perfectly, and His promises are fulfilled. We're going to keep pounding this drum every week: Missional motherhood is about Jesus.

Another of my prayers is that through the Old Testament overview you would see the grand plan of God to save a people for Himself, and in seeing God's heart of mercy, that your own heart would respond in worship.

Thinking back to the overview in the Session 2 video, what stood out as the major themes in the storyline?

Was there a theme in particular that really made you think of, piqued your curiosity about, or warmed your heart's affections for our great God? Explain.

How did Adam and Eve, the patriarchs, and the children of Israel respond to God when they realized (or failed to realize) that they were a part of God's big story?

used the "unlikelies" Cubs ☺

What thoughts come to your mind when you think of how God has written you into His story?

Imagine a 4-year-old child has just asked you the question, "Why did God make people?" What would you say?

sharing ✱ An exciting part of my conversations with my neighbors from around the world begins with a statement like this: "Christianity is probably not about what you think it is about." Then to confirm that statement, I ask them what they think Christianity is about. Most often they respond that our faith is just like theirs— just another way to be a good person. At this point I say, "Actually, Christianity says that none of us are good. But, there is one Man in the history of the world who was good." If they are curious to hear more, then I share with them God's big story, starting from the beginning. It may not be feasible to get through the whole story in one sitting, but you can certainly get the conversation going.

✱ Jesus story book Bible → audible version

Who are the children, young women, and friends God has placed in your life who may be eager to hear this big story? What about the ones who may not be eager to hear it?

Pray that God would give you eyes to see opportunities to tell about the wonderful things He has done.

I pray that as you listened to the overview, you got a glimpse of the unified message of the Bible, and that there arose in you an insatiable hunger for it. It's impossible for us to dig deep into the whole story of Scripture during this six-session study. Therefore, if we want to see our lives transformed by the Word of God, then we need to be fed by His Word every day. And not just in little snack bites. We all know what happens when we forgo a real meal and say, "Oh, I'll just grab a little bag of pretzels for lunch." At least, I know what happens whenever I do that! I soon end up rummaging around in the cupboards for five more little snacks because I'm still hungry. Feasting on God's Word is more like an endlessly long and limitlessly exciting buffet line. You're not going to get to the bottom of the proverbial bag and be starving for more. God will feed you and keep feeding you. When we dive deep into God's Word, with the help of the Holy Spirit, transformation of our lives is certain. Everything in our lives is affected—the way we read the news headlines, the way we relate to our husbands if we are married, the way we pray, the way we mother our children, and the way we reach out to our neighbors.

Which passages in the Old Testament are you eager to study more closely? Why?

I hope that as you listened to the overview of God's story, you clearly heard Jesus' invitation to make much of Him in all of life and in all the world. Jesus is progressively reestablishing His kingdom in our world that is rife with sin and chaos—His kingdom is coming! But as busy women, the approaching kingdom is obscured by all of the details of our days and nights. Our vision is clouded by the work of getting everyday things done every single day, putting out fires, and looking ahead to short-term goals. But all of these things are wrapped up in eternity—all of our work is meaningful because we do it as unto the Lord Jesus.

Thinking of the everyday ministry of motherhood as worship may be a new concept for some. For others, it may be an oft-forgotten fact. We all need reminders. In our first personal study time this week, we looked briefly at Colossians 3:1-4, where Paul reminded the church of the big picture. In the middle of that chapter there is a list of "ands" for us to remember to do (vv. 14-17). Paul sounded like a wise and concerned father, making sure his children don't forget what they need to know before they walk out the front door and face the world. At the end of his list of "ands," we read this catch-all reminder:

> *And whatever you do, in word or deed, do everything in the name of the Lord Jesus, giving thanks to God the Father through him.*

COLOSSIANS 3:17

READ COLOSSIANS 3:1-17 THREE TIMES TO GET A GRASP ON THE FLOW OF THE TEXT. Based on what you know about God's mission to glorify Himself in all the earth, how do all of these nitty-gritty details of Christian behavior fit into the big picture? How does Colossians 3:17 fit into the big picture?

We all need reminders! What will you do today to remind yourself (or remind a friend) of the mercy of God displayed in His desire to use our missional motherhood to glorify Himself?

THREE

In the Session 1 video, I hinted at the foundational concept that we are God's image bearers. Then, in the second video, I expanded it into a few more sentences. Now, in this personal study, we're going to look more deeply at what the Bible says about God's creation of image bearers.

Before God created everything, there were no created things. The triune God existed before and outside of His creation—perfectly happy, in perfect fellowship, and needing nothing. And then, God spoke. Out of nothing, God created everything we can see and everything we can't see. God's creation was good.

On the sixth day, God fashioned living, breathing images of Himself—male and female He created them. I know you may be very familiar with the text we're about to discuss, but refreshers are always helpful!

READ GENESIS 1. Then read verses 26-28 three times. What stands out as distinct in God's creation of man? List 5 observations (or more!).

NOW READ GENESIS 2 IN ITS ENTIRETY THREE TIMES. This is a more detailed account of the creation of man and woman. What stands out as distinct in God's creation of man according to this detailed account? List 5 observations (or more!).

COMPARE GENESIS 2:7 AND GENESIS 2:19. What differences do you notice between the man and the other living creatures?

This is curious, isn't it? The Creator stooped down to scoop up some earth, personally craft His own image, and animate His image bearer with His own breath. The other living creatures were formed out of the ground (Gen. 2:19), but the man, we're told, was the one in whom God breathed His breath of life. We should not think of God's "breath" as just oxygen. We breathe oxygen. But so do cheetahs, blue whales, slugs, and parakeets. Did the animals receive God's breath, too? No, they just have zoo breath. The word in Hebrew here is *ruah*, which can denote *spirit, wind,* and *breath* (depending on the context). To summarize the majority of the explanations given by biblical scholars, this *ruah* that God breathed into the first man is the same *ruah* that resurrected the lifeless bodies in the Valley of Dry Bones (Ezek. 37:9-10), and the same *ruah* which Jesus breathed on His disciples when He said, "Receive the Holy Spirit" (John 20:22). God's breath alone made Adam "a living soul" (1 Cor. 15:45, NASB). We are not fully alive unless the Spirit is in us. The creation account shows that it is God who gives life to our souls.

Adam and Eve were image bearers of the uncreated Creator, not of any other created thing. *Imaging* (in the verb sense of the word) is living and acting in a certain way because of the image we bear. Imaging God, then, is living in a way where we bear and reflect God's image. In layman's terms, to image something means to resemble and represent. The Reformed confessions describe being made in God's image as being like Him in His knowledge, righteousness, and holiness.[1] In addition to the "being" aspect of imaging God, Genesis describes a functional aspect of imaging God. You may have heard the term "vice regent" applied to Adam and Eve. It was like God put tiny statue-like representations of Himself in the middle of the garden in the middle of the world in the middle of the creation He made.

> *The image of God has been the subject of many scholarly discussions and doctoral dissertations. So, let's take it up for discussion, too! In your own words, what does it mean be made in the image of God? (Although the Bible doesn't really give us a cut-and-dry definition, look at Genesis 1:26-28 and note the clues given in this image-bearing creation declaration. You can also read Colossians 3:10 and Ephesians 4:24 for further study.)*

God fashioned living, breathing images of Himself—male and female He created them. The man and the woman lived in the garden God created for them, and they were given a purpose. Their purpose was to live by every word that proceeds from the mouth of God, multiply into more godly image bearers, and subdue the wilderness beyond the garden. In doing so, God's children would expand the dwelling place of God across the entire earth.

Based on your reflections on this passage in Genesis, what is God's revealed purpose for our motherhood?

So many things we do in our mothering/nurturing work fall under this umbrella—living by God's Word, multiplying image bearers (procreation, adoption, discipleship), and thereby expanding the dwelling place of God (ie., the Spirit-indwelled body of Christ). You could probably make a list of a thousand things that God enables you to do in this regard! But for the sake of time, just list 10.

Have you thought about those listed tasks or responsibilities in that way before? Have you ever considered that God is enabling you to do them because it is according to His purpose in creating you? Explain.

How does this view encourage you today? How will it change the way you go about these tasks and responsibilities in the future?

While we may be in agreement mentally with what Scripture says about motherhood, we all have "functional purpose statements" for our mothering work. In other words, we say one thing and we do another. "Yes, Lord! You created us for Your glory," we agree. But we're sinners, so we need regular reminders to walk in repentance toward God. One of the common sin struggles that nurturing women tend to have is that while we may agree that our role as nurturing women is to multiply God's image bearers through procreation, adoption, and discipleship, we treat those ministries as opportunities to multiply our own image. We work hard to exalt ourselves through our children and disciples when we ought to labor for God's glory instead.

> *Considering the selfish tendencies that cause our mothering work to go awry from God's purpose, are there things you need to repent of? Meditate on Psalm 139, asking God to search your heart and see if there is any way in you that grieves His Holy Spirit. Ask Him to lead you in the way everlasting.*

1. Westminster Shorter Catechism (WORDSearch Corp, 2003), Q.10.

FOUR

So far in our personal study this week we've reflected on God's big story as told in the Old Testament. Then, in Colossians 3, we looked briefly at God's calling for us to live according to the new creation that Jesus inaugurated through His death and resurrection. In the last section, we looked at God's design for humanity and His purpose for us according to Genesis 1 and 2.

The concept we're trying to dig into this week is how the facts of God's creation and re-creation informs our worldview, changes our minds, thrills our hearts, and strengthens our hands for the everyday ministry of motherhood. It bears repeating that we need to know about God's creation design and His new creation work in our lives through the gospel. We're pressing in to the Bible to see a distinctly Christian perspective of motherhood.

To further illustrate our need to view motherhood through a distinctly Christian perspective, I want to tell you about two of my friends. Janet* left her home country to find work, and now she works twelve-hour shifts, six days a week at the laundry shop downstairs. She lives in a one-bedroom apartment with fifteen other women. They've all moved to this city for the same purpose: to earn money in order to send it home to feed hungry mouths, to build homes, and to care for aging parents. Amy* lives in our building, and her family fled their home country just in time before their dictator was removed from power and executed. She is thankful to live in this peaceable country with her family, and she is elated that her kids can attend school without fear. I'll never forget the morning we heard that President Obama had been re-elected. I was visiting with Amy when the news was announced on her TV. She turned to me and said, "Congratulations on your country's peaceful election. Everyone can vote without being slaughtered on the way."

My friends do not know Jesus (yet). Though they feel some incentive to live for the next world, the particular afterlife they are hoping for does not exist. Day in and day out, they're just living for another day and another way to provide for the ones they love. This is a noble mission. But the mission of their sacrificial nurturing work would be radically reoriented if they understood that Christ is the

* Names have been changed.

Creator of motherhood. Motherhood is for His purposes in the world. The goal of motherhood is to exalt Him.

It is Christ's image that we are to embody as we plant the fields, judge the cases, fly the planes, organize the data, paint the paintings, feed the hungry, sweep the kitchen, pave the roads, diaper the babies, build the cities … and resist evil. As we embody Christ's image, we point to Him. In the minutes it took you to read those few paragraphs above, billions of image bearers received God's common grace as they walked through their days. Some woke up to a new day in which the sun has risen again. Some fell asleep under a sky filled with stars, smog, monsoon rain, or dust again.

Just one of the ways we glorify God as His dependent creatures is to praise Him even as we suffer. Suffering is a characteristic of this distinctly Christian nurturing that we're talking about. Only women who are born again in Jesus can nurture life in the face of death and in the face of their own death (as He did), while giving glory to God.

When we image Christ in this way, what we are doing is supernatural ministry. We die to self for His will and His purpose to be accomplished. You may think you are laboring to give birth to that baby, or filling out that adoption paperwork, or counseling the young lady at work by the sweat of your brow. But however sweaty your nurturing work may be (and mothering others can be sweaty work!), it is the Spirit of God who works through you.

> *What sort of deaths-to-self mothering work have you experienced this week?*

> *When we acknowledge that these things listed above are ultimately about who Jesus is and the purpose for which He has created our mothering, how does that change the way we think about the people we serve?*

The reality of suffering leads us to question ourselves. We all tend to want to walk on the sunnier, less rocky side of the path. We think that our work is invalid or not worthwhile when we are met with hardships or difficulties. Also, the presence of suffering comes into conflict with our desire to be validated and approved in our everyday ministry of motherhood. Personally, there are times when I have felt insecure about the things I do (and don't do) for my kids, my lost neighbors, and the ladies who are my fellow church members. If a mothering task or responsibility is hard for me to do for whatever reason, then I prefer to do anything but that! Actually, in those circumstances what I really want to do is whatever I think will get me some recognition—from my husband, kids, or whomever is watching.

Do you find that you struggle with similar insecurities in your nurturing work? Explain.

These issues are addressed throughout Paul's second letter to the church at Corinth, which is a heart-felt missionary support letter. Paul wanted his readers to see how God Himself was the One who had commended him to minister to them. The apostle desired for the people to support his faithful ministry to even more Gentiles. In the letter, Paul was not sinfully asking to be praised by the people he served; he was describing to them the joy they would have as they affirmed his gospel ministry. Paul wasn't confused as to what he ought to be doing; he explained the nature and goal of his service. He shared this out of his love for the people. This love resembles that of a discerning and selfless mother who sees what is good for her kids and wants her kids to embrace that good.

Let's look at the first verses in 2 Corinthians, shall we? In his introduction, Paul defended his ministry and apostleship. His readers could know he was the real deal because he was really, truly suffering for their sakes. Suffering was happening, but Paul was undaunted in his ministry.

READ THROUGH 2 CORINTHIANS 1:1-11 THREE TIMES. What did God do for Paul and his coworkers as they were suffering?

What did Paul say was one of the purposes for his suffering (v. 4)?

What is the correlation between Christ's sufferings and Christ's comfort (v. 5)?

What is the correlation between the suffering and comfort of Paul and his companions and the suffering and comfort of the people (v. 7)?

In what ways do mothers and nurturers suffer as they minister to others?

In what ways do mothers and nurturers receive comfort from Christ?

Perhaps you have heard this phrase: "God won't give you more than you can handle." Maybe a well-meaning friend even said this to you during a difficult time. How does this Scripture passage speak to this idea?

God's design for our mothering, discipling work is outward to bless others and God-ward to give Him glory. Our mothering and discipling are not inward endeavors where we work to amass approval and recognition for ourselves from our kids, husband, the church, or the world. God gets the glory, and we receive comfort from Him. As we go about the good work God has designed for us (and designed us for), we suffer many afflictions. It is out of the comfort we receive from Christ that we mother and disciple others.

> *Give examples from your own life of how you have suffered, been comforted by Jesus, and were then able to minister to others out of that Christ-shared comfort.*

Meditating on how Paul shared in both Christ's sufferings and comforts brings us tremendous encouragement as nurturing women. There is no denying that our ministry is difficult at times and that the comforts the world offers us are useless and empty. We need Christ! And what a joy it is to see that He has designed us to not only need Him for our mothering work, but to also image Him as we labor to make disciples.

There's so much more to say about how God has created mothering to glorify Himself. I'll speak to that in the Session 3 video.

NEW CREATION LIFE IN CHRIST IS THE NEW NORMAL

REVIEW

Welcome to Session 3 of *Missional Motherhood*! Let's begin by reviewing your homework from last week.

With Colossians 3:1-4 in mind, how would you answer someone who asked you, "How do you do what you do?"

Who are the children, young women, and friends whom God has placed in your life who may be eager to hear this big story? Who are the ones you think may not be eager to hear?

What does it mean to be made in the image of God? How would a correct understanding of the image of God transform the way your culture views motherhood?

What is Christ's purpose for our thousands of little "deaths-to-self" each and every day as we go about our work of making disciples?

Do you agree with the phrase, "God won't give you more than you can handle"? Explain. How does 2 Corinthians 1:1-11 speak to this?

If you are willing, share with the group a time when you suffered, were comforted by Jesus, and were then able to minister to others out of that Christ-shared comfort?

WATCH

Use the space below to take notes on the Session 3 video.

DISCUSS

Use the following questions to debrief the teaching from the Session 3 video.

Explain Seasonal Obsessive Disorder. Do you ever suffer from it? Describe your life when that happens.

What did Gloria mean when she said, "The missional vision of our motherhood, with its sights set on the return of Christ, reminds us that we are all currently in the season of life"?

How does understanding your permanent position of being "in Christ" change the way you view the season of life you are in right now?

Some of the Jews in Jesus' day would have been happy to simply be rescued from Rome. Is there a "Rome" in your life that distracts you from waiting for your ultimate deliverance? Explain.

Name one area of weakness in your life that serves as a witness to others because Christ uses it to show His perfect power.

CLOSE

Lead each person in your group to choose a partner. Direct the pairs to pray for one another about how God would use them—weaknesses and all—in the lives of their children, friends, family, and neighbors to shine the light of Christ.

ONE

In the Session 3 video, I laid out a defense of why new creation life in Christ is our new normal. It's the eternal season of life that all Christians are in. And this season of life in Christ colors and informs and empowers every temporary season of life we will ever experience.

For the next two weeks we're going to step back to take in the panoramic view of another theme that shows up throughout the whole Bible. It's a sweeping theme that appears in every genre and in many familiar passages. This theme seems to illuminate the tapestry of God's big story with a peculiarly beautiful light. It is unique. In my experience of talking with people from different world religions, I haven't heard anyone mention anything similar to this amazing work of God.

We'll take what we see in this big picture and zoom in to apply it to our motherhood. So just by way of reminder, here are two helpful application questions to keep in mind as you complete your personal study:

How does this truth show me where motherhood fits into God's mission?

How does this truth strengthen my faith for the everyday ministry of motherhood (raising children, discipleship, service) that God has given me?

I'm so excited about this theme, because I've seen God bear tremendous fruit in my life as I grow in my understanding of it. And so, without further ado, the theme we're looking at this week is the priesthood.

What are your first impressions of this topic?

I imagine the answers will vary depending on the religious backgrounds and life experiences of everyone in your group.

We see shadows of Christ throughout the theme of the priesthood, both in the Old and New Testaments. Beyond the shadows, we see Christ Himself, our "great high priest who has ascended into heaven" (Heb. 4:14, NIV). Understanding priests and priesthood requires explanation from Scripture because many world religions have priests, and even in broader Christianity there are misconceptions about the subject. However, biblical priesthood is distinct and has tremendous bearing on our missional motherhood.

> *What are some examples of priesthoods (formal or functional) that you see in your community and culture?*

We're going to dig into the big story of the Bible this week, focusing specifically on this topic in order gain clarity, receive encouragement for our mothering ministry, and adore the person of Jesus Christ. Let's go back to the beginning, shall we? In Genesis 1:26-28, we find the foundation for our priestly work. We remember that God created man and woman in His image, giving us dominion over the earth and a charge to multiply image bearers to fill the world He created. In the next chapter of Genesis, we see a more detailed account of the creation of humans.

> *READ GENESIS 2:15. What two tasks did God give to Adam?*

God walked among His people in the garden of Eden (Gen. 3:8), fellowshiping with them until they broke that fellowship through their rebellion against Him. Because of Adam and Eve's sin, all their offspring would be enemies of God, born into sin, and unable to please Him.

> *How does sin frustrate our nurturing work?*

> *How does this frustration hit close to home for you?*

Generation after generation of sinful, work-frustrated, image bearers were born. Sin multiplied as the image bearers multiplied, and then God cleansed the earth with a flood (Gen. 6–9). Remember that the survivors were not cleansed of their sin, however. Then, the people gathered to use their God-given skills and abilities to build a monument to exalt themselves. However, God judged their arrogance and pride, scattering and dividing them at the Tower of Babel (Gen. 11). Following this action, God chose an elderly couple to be His people. God made Abraham a promise: "And I will make of you a great nation, and I will bless you and make your name great, so that you will be a blessing" (Gen. 12:2). The Abrahamic covenant clearly reiterated that God had not abandoned His plan to use men and women in His mission to the world, and that He would choose to use whomever He desired.

This truth leads us to examine our own hearts. As women who work hard to serve others day and night, we tend to forget that we have this opportunity because of God's mercy to us. From the children underfoot or away at school to the ladies we disciple and witness to in the workplace and community, our nurturing work is a gift. We all have a need to repent of our feelings of entitlement. We do not deserve to be used by God. We do not deserve to be ambassadors of Christ in our homes, workplaces, neighborhoods, or generations. We do not deserve to be given spiritual gifts with which to serve the church. We do not deserve to be included in God's mission to the world, period.

Yet, it pleases Him to include us.

Take a moment right now to sit in awe of God's kindness to you—that He would save you, give you a mission, equip you for ministry, and surround you with people to serve on Christ's behalf. Journal your reflections in the space below.

Abraham didn't deserve to be chosen to be a blessing to the whole world. He and his sons lived and died in faith, believing God's promise even though they didn't receive (in their earthly lives) the things they were promised. Instead, they saw the promises fulfilled by faith "and greeted them from afar, and having acknowledged that they were strangers and exiles on the earth" (Heb. 11:13).

While they lived as slaves in Egypt, the nation of Israel multiplied. Then God delivered His "firstborn" (Ex. 4:22-23) out of slavery through doorways covered in blood and through walls made of sea water. Once the Israelites were on the other side of the Red Sea, something significant happened. God called Moses to meet with Him on Mount Sinai to tell the people what His plans were for them. This was "mission rebooted," but not like anyone had ever seen before. We'll pick up at that part of our story in the next personal study session.

TWO

You have probably heard the saying, "God does not have a Plan B." It sounds trite and truncated, but it is true.

I'm about to ask you a series of really personal questions, and you may not feel ready to share with others what you are feeling and thinking. If that's the case, then you don't have to write anything down, but ponder your answers in your heart.

Do you ever wish you were someone else or lived a different life? Perhaps you have resented how God made you or how He didn't make you? The children or family He gave you or didn't give you? The people you are called to serve or wish you were called to serve?

If this is or has been your struggle, take heart; you are not alone. In fact, we see similar struggles in the Bible. God knows the dissatisfaction and discontentment about our sinful humanity, and He still has compassion on us. Just as He has no Plan B for His mission to fill the earth with His glory, He has no Plan B for our individual lives. He is pleased to be glorified through us even when we are not pleased to be who He made us or live in the circumstances He has orchestrated.

What happened at Sinai is a colorful illustration of God's deliberate, unfailing plan to fill the earth with His glory through His people. A nation of former slaves who were homeless and weak set up camp at the foot of the mountain. Moses went up the mountain to meet with God. And would you believe what God said?

READ EXODUS 19:3-6. Remembering Israel's history, what was the nation like when God delivered them from Egypt?

What did God say He would make the nation to be?

What did God say would be Israel's responsibility?

Considering Israel's earlier actions, how likely were they to be obedient to God's call? Explain your answer.

Wow. God came to commit Himself to a bunch of grouchy-pants complainers and turn them into an entire kingdom of commissioned priests. But when the people heard the thunder and the trumpet and saw the smoke and clouds, they shrank back from letting God speak to them (Ex. 20:18-21). Later, we see where the people were to remain at the foot of the mountain, while the priests and 70 elders went a short distance up the mountain. Then Moses went on alone up Mount Sinai to meet with God and receive God's good Law for the people (Ex. 24). Afterward, "Moses came and told the people all the words of the LORD and all the rules. And all the people answered with one voice and said, 'All the words that the LORD has spoken we will do'" (Ex. 24:3). Moses performed a blood ceremony with the blood of sacrificed animals and said, "Behold the blood of the covenant that the LORD has made with you in accordance with all these words" (Ex. 24:8). And there you have it—a covenant between Yahweh and His people.

Can you relate to the Israelites who didn't want to meet with God and were terrified to let God speak to them as a kingdom of priests and a holy nation? Why or why not?

Can you relate to the Israelites who were optimistic that they would obey "all the words that the LORD has spoken"? Why or why not?

For the next 40 days and 40 nights, Moses was in the midst of the swirling smoke and consuming fire of Sinai as God wrote down His commandments on tablets of stone for the peoples' instruction. On that mountain, Yahweh revealed to Moses the things He planned to use in order to facilitate His relationship to His people. He is I AM, the Holy One of Israel. He gave Moses instructions for His tabernacle and the ark. Wait. What? His tabernacle? A dwelling place for God among men? Yes, that's right. This good news must have shocked the people to their core.

> READ EXODUS 29:42-46. What was God going to do at the tent of meeting (tabernacle)?

> What was God going to do to the tent of meeting?

> What was God going to do to Aaron and his sons?

> What reason did God give for dwelling among the people of Israel?

God would walk among His people again! In His mercy, our holy God ordained a way that He might dwell among His now fallen people without compromising His utter holiness. That means was the tabernacle. We, who have the indwelling Spirit now, should sober our hearts in wonder at this. How easily we forget. How presumptuous we often are. "God is with you!" we quip, and indeed, God is with us. But His presence among us came at a price that none of us could have paid.

Are you certain that God is with you in your motherhood? What difference would it make today if you were absolutely certain, beyond a shadow of a doubt that God is with you as you make disciples in your home, neighborhood, and this world?

THREE

Do you remember what Adam's two tasks were in the garden of Eden (Gen. 2:15)? Theologian G.K. Beale has pointed out that those same two Hebrew verbs from Genesis 2:15 appear together elsewhere in the Old Testament.[1] In Numbers 3, God commissioned Aaron and his sons as priests to serve in the tabernacle, and He commissioned the tribe of Levi to be the priestly tribe. There are priestly duties that go along with this special role; it was no mere ceremonial figurehead. You don't just wear the religious garb and put a new business card in your wallet. Being a priest meant there were corresponding job duties and ministries.

READ NUMBERS 3:5-8. What tasks did God give to the priests?

The verb translated *work* in the Genesis 2:15 passage is the same as the verb translated *minister/serve* in the Numbers 3:5-8 passage. Likewise, the verb translated *keep* in the Genesis 2:15 passage is the same as the verb translated *guard* in the Numbers 3:5-8 passage.

What was Adam's work?

What was the priests' ministry/service?

What was Adam supposed to keep? Why?

What were the priests charged with guarding? Why?

It looked like everything sad was becoming untrue for the Hebrews. Their backs, bent over from generations of slave labor, began to straighten. They were on their way to the land God promised them—at last! God told them repeatedly, "And I will walk among you and will be your God, and you shall be my people" (Lev. 26:12). It looked like everything from that moment on was going to be different.

But their hearts were still turned in on themselves. Time and again, while they trekked across the desert, they grumbled against God, the One who had rescued them, and quarreled against Moses, the leader whom God had appointed. Half of Exodus could be hashtagged #smh ("shaking my head" for non-Twitter folks). What happened in a wilderness far, far away (well, not far at all from where I'm writing right now!) seems to us like an obscure historical incident. Regardless of where you are living, though, this scene hits so close to home it's not funny. God feeds us with bread from heaven and water from rocks, but we're not happy unless we have whatever it is they have over there. Our hearts need renewal.

Have you felt like parts of your own walk with God could be hashtagged #smh? That God would be delighted to use you in ministry except for _____?

God is faithful to His name even though we are not! How have you seen the Lord work in and through you despite your weaknesses and failings?

Take a moment right now to thank God for His kindness to you and repent of any sin that He graciously brings to your mind.

This is the reality that we, our children, and our neighbors face. Apart from the saving grace of God, we are prone to wander from Him. When my child grumbles against me, I can sympathize with her because I, too, know what it feels like to question God's authority in my life and grumble against His wisdom. When my neighbor does not appreciate the truth I share with her about God, I can sympathize with her because I, too, scoffed at God before He changed my heart. We are powerless to save our children and our friends. And because we are powerless, we call on the One who is all-powerful and mighty to save. We pray that light would dawn in their hearts. "Let Your light shine into darkness, Lord!" We pray that the Spirit would open their eyes. And we pray that the Lord would incline their hearts toward Him when they see Him. We pray they would not make excuses for themselves and their sin, but that they would repent and cast themselves on the mercy of our loving and forgiving God who sent His Son to pay for our sin on the cross.

Write down the names of five non-believing friends or family members whom you want to pray for more regularly and talk with about Christ.

I encourage you to ask the Lord to help you in this endeavor. I've often prayed this: "Father, my spirit is willing but my flesh is weak. Help me pray for this person—lead me in prayer for them often. Make me bold to speak to them about You."

How are you planning to follow through with your desire to pray for others and share Christ with them?

As we discussed in the previous homework, we need heart renewal if we are to live lives that are pleasing to the Lord. Without God's gracious drawing of our hearts, we are all prone to wander from Him, not to Him. The entropy of our hearts is like the state of the living room on a day when the kids are off from school. It just naturally tends to get messier, not more orderly. We need to be changed from the inside out.

As a consequence of his own rebellion against God, Moses was not allowed to enter the promised land with the remnant of God's people. However, before he died in the wilderness, Moses gave final instructions and warnings to this new generation. Foreseeing the days when they would repeat the sins of their parents, Moses prophesied that God would scatter them in exile. (See Deut. 28–29.)

Recall Israel's calling in Exodus 19:6. What were they supposed to be and do?

But what did their king lead them to do generations later, according to 2 Chronicles 33:9?

Not only did Moses prophesy the people's deportation from the land, but he also foresaw how the Lord God would mercifully bring them back from the places to which they would be scattered (Deut. 30:1-4). From among all the peoples of the earth and even "if your outcasts are in the uttermost parts of heaven, from there the LORD your God will gather you, and from there he will take you" (Deut. 30:4). This gathering of God's people would be global in scope, and their restoration would be comprehensive. Just look at what God promises next.

READ DEUTERONOMY 6:5-7. Now flip forward a few pages to read God's promise in Deuteronomy 30:6. Compare these two passages. What is the same? What is different?

We cannot compare that promise to any promise made to us from another person, even if he or she has the best of intentions to follow through on big plans. God's promise is what you would call a "game changer." Because God always keeps His promises, and this promise addresses our deep need for permanent, spiritual renewal, we can have hope for tomorrow and grace for today.

Take some time in prayer right now to praise God for His unfailing commitment to finish the good work He has started in us individually and corporately as His blood-bought people.

1. G. K. Beale, *The Temple and the Church's Mission: A Biblical Theology of the Dwelling Place of God* (Downers Grove, IL: IVP Academic, 2004).

FOUR

We need hope for tomorrow and grace for today. We need God to change us from the inside out if we are to be Christ's hands and feet and mouthpiece in the world we live in. The prophet Jeremiah took up this theme in what scholars like to call the "Book of Consolation," a unique set of four chapters (Jer. 30–33) which speaks to a breathtaking, unprecedented, future restoration. He prophesied in the last days just before Jerusalem fell to the Babylonians in 586 B.C., but there were other "last days" on his mind—the last days in which we are now living post-Easter. In the middle of the Book of Consolation is God's announcement of a new covenant.

READ JEREMIAH 31:31-34. Name the differences the Lord describes between the Mosaic covenant and this new covenant.

God is going to write His law straight onto human hearts. That is amazing! Every single person who is included in the people of God will truly know Him. God will forgive our iniquity and remember our sin no more. This is worth repeating and rephrasing for ourselves a hundred times—what grace we have been shown through Jesus, the One who established this new covenant!

Here's how I have rephrased Jeremiah 31:31-34 to teach the concept of the new covenant to my children and non-believing neighbors: God made a new covenant in which our sins are wiped away from His memory, and He gives us new hearts that are inclined to love Him back because His Spirit lives in us. Jesus' sacrifice on the cross makes this happen for anyone, regardless of their ethnicity.

Let's look at one more Old Testament passage about what this new covenant entails.

READ JOEL 2:28-29. On whom will God pour out His Spirit? Will any believers be excluded for their age, gender, or economic status?

NOW READ ACTS 2:1-47. What events take place in this passage? How was Joel's prophecy fulfilled?

In the new covenant, we have become a kingdom of priests! This is distinct from the Mosaic covenant days, where only priests and prophets taught the people (and of course, parents taught their children about God's law—see Deut. 6:7). With God's law now written on our new, circumcised hearts, not only do we have a saving knowledge of God by His grace, but we all have an empowered role to pass on this gospel to others through evangelism, discipleship, and missions. God has made us a priesthood of believers. This is far too wonder-filled for us to dream up on our own.

Along with this priestly status, we have corresponding privileges and responsibilities.

READ ACTS 1:1-11. Who is featured in this text? What are they doing (just a brief summary)?

What did Jesus say was the promise of the Father (vv. 4-5)?

What did the disciples want to know in verse 6?

Recall what you have already learned about the prophesies of the restoration. What might the disciples be looking forward to?

How did Jesus answer their question (v. 7)?

Write out Acts 1:8 in the space below.

What kind of power was Jesus referring to?

There is a kind of déjà vu going on here. The disciples had heard that phrase, "you will be my witnesses," in their readings in the Old Testament. And now they're hearing it applied to them, of all people!

> *LOOK UP ISAIAH 43:10-12. What did Yahweh say His people will know and bear witness to?*

There is no place excluded from the regions that Jesus included in Acts 1:8. When He said, "to the end of the earth," there is really no way around the all-encompassing reach of such a statement. Jesus really was claiming to be God. He really was announcing that His disciples are His [i.e., God's] witnesses. And He really was claiming that His dominion includes the entire world.

> *READ DANIEL 7:9-14. Daniel had been given a vision of the heavenly throne room and the future that is to come. What he saw and heard absolutely boggles the mind. Who is present in this vision?*

Zooming in on verse 13, "one like a son of man" is presented to the Ancient of Days. This One is the second person of the Trinity, the eternal Son of God. He is the Son who became God incarnate: Christ Jesus.

According to verse 14, what is given to Jesus?

Who serves Him?

What is His dominion like? What is His kingdom like?

Given this description of Jesus' dominion and kingdom, what kind of confidence and encouragement can His servants have as they serve Him?

How can this particular vision of the risen Christ change the way you see your mothering ministry right now?

How can this particular hope "globalize" the way you see your mothering ministry? Do you see how the work you do has potential to impact the world? Explain.

In John's apocalyptic vision in Revelation, he saw and heard that Jesus Christ has successfully fulfilled every promise of God, including the promise to make for Himself a kingdom of priests and a holy nation! Look at these amazing verses.

READ REVELATION 1:1-6. What has Jesus done?

Because of what Jesus has done, what does He deserve?

NOW READ ALL OF REVELATION 5. What has Jesus done?

Because of what Jesus has done, what does He deserve?

From where do the "kingdom and priests" in Revelation 5:10 come? (Hint: Look at verse 9.)

These people who were ransomed for God from every tribe, language, people, and nation have been made a kingdom of priests, a strikingly beautiful, multi-colored, pan-ethnic people. Their role, as the text says, is to reign on the earth as a kingdom of priests to God. Finally.

Theirs is the privileged position of seeing God face-to-face as Moses did, a privilege that even the high priest, Aaron, was never given. "They will see his face, and his name will be on their foreheads" (Rev. 22:4). The kingdom of priests will serve God in eternity, reigning forever and ever (Rev. 22:5). And by "their foreheads," He means "ours"—all those who are repenting of their sin and calling on the name of Jesus to be saved.

How does this vision of the risen, ascended, and exalted Christ cast out any fears you have about:
- *the sacrifices you are making in your mothering?*

- *the temptations you are facing to present the ministry God has given you?*

- *the suffering you are anticipating or experiencing as you serve others?*

THE PRIESTESS
NEXT DOOR

REVIEW

Welcome to Session 4 of *Missional Motherhood*! Let's begin by reviewing your homework from last week.

How does sin frustrate your nurturing work?

Are you certain that God is with you in your motherhood? What difference would it make today if you were absolutely certain beyond a shadow of a doubt that God is with you as you make disciples in your home, neighborhood, and this world?

How are you planning to follow through with your desire to pray for others and share Christ with them?

Acts 1:8 lists four geographic regions—how does this correspond to circumstances in your life?

Recall our study in the Daniel 7 and Revelation 1 passages. He is the Lord to whom salvation belongs! How do those visions of the risen and enthroned Christ encourage you as you make disciples?

How can this particular hope "globalize" the way you see your mothering ministry? Do you see how the work you do has potential to impact the world? Explain.

WATCH

Use the space below to take notes on the Session 4 video.

2 Chron.

DISCUSS

Use the following questions to debrief the teaching from the Session 4 video.

Most women have felt frustration over their everyday mothering ministry, wondering if it matters in eternity. Imagine you are sitting on the couch with a mom who is struggling with this. How would you encourage her?

God has qualified us for the priestly ministry He has called us to. In what ways are you tempted to think you are not qualified? How does 1 Peter 2 correct that thinking?

We must connect our faith to our everyday lives. Is this something you need help doing? Explain. How can you get that help? How can you help others connect their faith to their everyday lives?

Are you a member of a local body of Christ? What are some ways you can use your gifts to build up the members of your church?

CLOSE

Lead each person in your group to choose a partner. Direct the pairs to discuss the obstacles they face in living out their identities as part of Christ's pan-ethnic, multicolored, diversely gifted, holy priesthood of believers. Encourage them to share specific personal requests and intercede for each other.

ONE

This personal study begins our second week of exploring the subject of the priesthood and how it transforms the way we look at our mothering ministries.

> *Let's get right into it, shall we?*
> *REREAD 1 PETER 2:1-10.*

Now, let's focus on one verse, 1 Peter 2:5.

In our priestly status we have received the privilege of offering spiritual sacrifices that are acceptable to God through Jesus Christ. That is astonishing! I cannot tell you how many times I feel as though the ministry I do for my kids and neighbors is trivial or pointless. Do you ever feel the same way?

> *What do you do when your everyday ministry of motherhood feels trivial or pointless?*

For me, I tend to daydream about all the things I'd rather be doing, and sometimes I do those things instead of what God has put in front of me to do to serve my family and neighbors.

> *What wrong advice does the world offer to women who feel like their work is pointless?*

> *How does this hinder rather than strengthen our faith for our nurturing ministries?*

The Bible has a different word to say to our untrustworthy feelings. (God's Word has a wonderfully convicting way of doing that!) I've listed some verses below that deal with the spiritual sacrifices that are pleasing to the Lord. Read each verse, then give an example of that kind of sacrifice from the lives of the missional mothers you know:

Philippians 2:17 (sacrificial offering of faith)

Philippians 4:18 (sacrificial giving)

Romans 12:1 (sacrificial living)

Hebrews 13:15 (sacrifice of praise)

Let's look at another verse: 1 Peter 2:9. I've written it below and highlighted the portion we're going to dig into:

> *But you are a chosen race, a royal priesthood, a holy nation, a people for his own possession, that you may proclaim the excellencies of him who called you out of darkness into his marvelous light.*
>
> **1 PETER 2:9**

This calling to proclaim is the prophetic aspect of our priestly ministry. (When you see the term *prophetic* in this study, think "telling forth God's truth," not "fore-telling God's truth.") Our proclamation of God's excellence and work is part of our privileged responsibility as witnesses and members of Christ's royal priesthood. God chose to make us all of these things listed in 1 Peter 2:9 so that we may proclaim. Now, I know that some of you may be feeling like Moses at this point, about to insist that God raise up somebody else to speak His truth. If that's you, I want to take a moment to encourage you that the ministry God has called you to is, by nature, supernatural. God is delighted to have His excellencies proclaimed through people who feel they have little-to-no natural ability. God uses the weak things of the world to show that He is doing that which only He can do—the supernatural. God is calling dead people out of darkness into His marvelous light. You can't do that for your kids; only God can. You can't do that for your neighbors; only God can. You can't do that for the lost people next door or around the world; only God can. Our role is to proclaim that He raises the dead; His role is to do the resurrection work.

You may still be persuaded that any type of ministry that involves speaking forth God's truth is not for you. What you want to proclaim is "Let someone who is more articulate do this—not me!" But let me assure you, if you have been born again into Christ and filled with His Spirit, Jesus wants to be glorified through your truth-telling. The Bible uses various terms for this prophetic ministry. I've listed some of them below. Perhaps these synonyms will sound similar to the nurturing words you speak each and every day to the people around you: exhorting, explaining, confessing, rebuking, announcing.

> *Can you think of any occasions this week when you have:*
>
> * *exhorted someone to stand firm in their faith?*
>
> * *explained God's truth to a child, disciple, or non-Christian?*
>
> * *confessed that Christ is Lord in the company of those who agree or even disagree?*
>
> * *rebuked someone who was stumbling in the throes of sin?*
>
> * *announced the good news to someone who needed to hear it?*

If so, my friend, then God is using you to proclaim His excellencies.

Sometimes when I walk around my neighborhood looking for friends to talk to, I may speak with someone using one or many of those prophetic activities. My husband jokes that this is a ministry of "intentional loitering." (Who knew that God would redeem those loitering skills that I perfected in the shopping mall during junior high!) You don't have to live in a busy city center in order to exhort your friends to believe the gospel, explain God's truths to the ignorant, confess that Christ is Lord, rebuke those who are dragging others down to death, and announce that there is forgiveness of sins through the cross. I wonder if any names or faces came to your mind as you read that short, bulleted list or considered the prophetic aspect of the priesthood Jesus has placed us in.

There are people whom God has placed in your life (this much is obvious). What is not as obvious to us, though, is that God is pleased to have chosen us for ministry in His name. We are easily distracted and discouraged little sheep. However, read back over 1 Peter 2:9, focusing on the first part of the verse.

God has chosen us to be a chosen race; Christians are "blood relatives" through Christ's blood. God has chosen us to be a royal priesthood; Christians are priests to God regardless of their jobs. God has chosen us to be a holy nation; Christians are citizens of the kingdom of God regardless of their passport. God has chosen us to be a people for His own possession; Christians are twice His—by nature of creation and through Christ's redeeming work. All this God has done for us and in us so that we may proclaim His excellencies. He is the One who called us out of darkness and into His marvelous light, and that is the message we proclaim, exhort others to believe, explain to those who don't understand, and confess in the public square.

> *It pleased the Lord to choose us for this calling to be lived out among specific people. List some of the people in your close proximity, some you love who are far away, and some you may not have met but God has placed on your heart.*

In our priestly role we mediate the love of Christ to His enemies. Some of His enemies will drop their weapons of unbelief and repent. Most of His enemies will remain opposed to Him. You don't know who the lost sheep are, but Jesus does. You don't know who will refuse to believe, and in hearing the good news will reject it and heap further

condemnation on themselves. Do not think it is a mere coincidence that the sovereign Christ has placed you where He has placed you. Your temporary season of life, your strengths and abilities, your weaknesses and faults, your physical location, and your relationships—all of these are part of Christ's intentional, strategic design to be exalted in all the earth through extending mercy to the lost sheep and judging those who reject Him.

Even when we are uncertain about our ministry, Christ is certain, and He will effectually call those who are His using us, His witnesses.

> And I have other sheep that are not of this fold. I must bring them also, and they will listen to my voice. So there will be one flock, one shepherd.

JOHN 10:16

Because Christ is sovereign, we have all been handed an Esther-like opportunity to magnify Christ in our lives "for such a time as this" (Esth. 4:14). God has given you those specific children and disciples with those needs for such a time as this. They need to know Christ and Him crucified—that is their most urgent need. Your friends need to know the One who fills all things. You are "the priest" next door to those neighbors. Christ has made you a priest and He has given you His authority to carry His message to a lost and dying world. Your ears may hear about a crisis a half a world away, and you may feel frustrated that you cannot go to them physically or send any aid yourself, but remember that you have direct access to the God who sits in the heavens, and you can plead for their souls.

Because of the sacrifice Jesus made on our behalf, we can have confidence in our evangelistic ministry. This is a blood-bought ministry—a privileged priesthood. But how quickly we downplay our mothering work, trivialize our ministry, and just plain forget to pray for God's will to be done on earth as it is in heaven. The doctrine of the priesthood of believers has greatly encouraged me, especially when it seems that what I do doesn't matter unless it is considered extraordinary in the eyes of the world. When I'm reminded of my position in the feel powerless or flippant about my negligence in prayer. Have you felt this way before? Friends, the power that we need for our missional motherhood is God's power. He is ready and willing to wield that power in accordance with His will.

John Newton wrote a hymn called, "Come, My Soul, Thy Suit Prepare,"[1] that has echoes of these themes. It would be worth your time to read the whole hymn, but for now, here are the first two stanzas for your encouragement:

Come, my soul, thy suit prepare,
Jesus loves to answer prayer,
He himself has bid thee pray,
Therefore will not say thee nay.

Thou art coming to a King,
Large petitions with thee bring;
For his grace and pow'r are such,
None can ever ask too much.

---

1. John Newton, "Come, My Soul, Thy Suit Prepare," *Olney Hymns* (London: W. Oliver, 1779), number 31, pg. 72.

TWO

"Do you ever sit down?"

Has anyone ever asked you that before? Sometimes it seems a mom works hard all day without a moment's rest. On crazy long days, I know that if I sit down it's not likely that I will get up again!

There were no chairs among the tabernacle furniture. The priests' work was never finished. There was always a lamp to trim, an animal to sacrifice, incense to burn, and on and on. Purification for sins was exhausting work for the priests, and they served in this manner for generations.

> READ HEBREWS 1:1-3. How does the text describe the person of Jesus?

> What does the text say that Jesus has done?

> After Jesus made purification for our sins, what did He do?

> What does this imply about the sacrifice Jesus made on the cross?

> What does it mean to you that Jesus is finished making purification for sins?

> How would it change the way you serve in ministry to your family and neighbors to remember that your sins have been fully paid for?

READ HEBREWS 2:17-18.

The writer of Hebrews speaks about Jesus' ability to help in the present tense because Jesus is alive, risen from the dead, and ascended into heaven. Because Jesus suffered when tempted, He is able to help those who are being tempted.

What are some common temptations for you as a mothering woman?

How does this knowledge about Christ suffering when tempted change the way you face those temptations?

How does this change the way you counsel others who are facing temptation?

Sometimes we look to others or to our accomplishments to commend ourselves before God. We may try to serve as our own functional priests, bringing our maternal accolades before the Lord to try to levy some kind of reward or exchange. We may try to justify ourselves through the opinions of others ("If she thinks I'm wonderful—I must be.")

READ HEBREWS 4:14-16. This passage speaks of Christ's utter legitimacy to be our advocate before God.

What are Jesus' priestly credentials according to these three verses?

According to verse 16, what should our response be? And what will the result be?

Remember how the Israelites refused to let God speak to them in Exodus 20? Is the situation still the same for us today? God in His holiness remains unchanged, of course. God is still utterly holy and cannot be in the presence of anything that is unclean. How has Jesus' work changed the way we approach God? These questions are discussed in Hebrews 12.

> READ HEBREWS 12:18-24. How does the writer describe the scene at Mount Sinai? Who is there? What are they experiencing?

> Verse 22 says, "But you have come to Mount Zion and to the city of the living God ..." Who is this "you"?

> Whom have you joined on the scene at Mount Zion?

> What does this passage say that Jesus is?

> What does it mean that Jesus is the mediator of a new covenant?

> Have you ever thought of yourself as being part of "the assembly of the firstborn who are enrolled in heaven"? What do you think this phrase means?

Coming to Mount Sinai and coming to Mount Zion are two totally different experiences, aren't they? In our evangelism we are pointing people to Jesus, the mediator of a new covenant. Through Him, people are able to come to Mount Zion. This is good news! The terrifying demands of God's perfect law could never be met by sinful men, women, and children. All of us would be dead where we stood, if we were to meet God face-to-face at the foot of Mount Sinai.

But Jesus made it possible for us to come to God. He fulfilled all that God's righteous commands required of Israel. Jesus is the true Israel and the mediator of a better covenant. In Christ's priesthood, He is able to stand in our place as the atoning sacrifice for our sin because His blood speaks a better word.

In Andrew Bonar's biography of Scottish minister Robert Murray M'Cheyne, he highlights a key aspect of M'Cheyne's view of Christ's intercessory work. These three short sentences carry with them a profoundly encouraging, emboldening, and strengthening thought. Read this quote aloud (it's OK if you're in a coffee shop or at the office, this truth can stir the hearts of everyone in earshot):

> "If I could hear Christ praying for me in the next room, I would not fear a million of enemies. Yet the distance makes no difference; he is praying for me."[1]

Now read this passage from Hebrews 7:23-25 aloud. (This will clarify the former quote.)

The former priests were many in number, because they were prevented by death from continuing in office, but he holds his priesthood permanently, because he continues forever. Consequently, he is able to save to the uttermost those who draw near to God through him, since he always lives to make intercession for them.

HEBREWS 7:23-25

We have assurance because of Christ that grace is what we will receive from the Father when we come to Him by way of the cross. Our position of nearness to God is secured by Christ, our great High Priest who enacted the new covenant in His own blood. Nothing but the blood of Jesus can do this for us or grant us this kind of expectation: "And this is the confidence that we have toward him, that if we ask anything according to his will he hears us" (1 John 5:14).

Journal a prayer, reflecting on the Scripture passages you've just read.

1. Andrew Bonar, *Memoir and Remains of the Rev. Robert Murray M'Cheyne* (London: Dundee, 1800), page 155.

THREE

There is no way we could pay God back for the gift He has given us in His Son. When I was in college Bible studies, we would put it this way: It's like God gives you a brand new car, and so you fish around in your pocket and pull out some fuzz, a couple of quarters, and a fast-food receipt. You hand it all to God and say, "That car must have set you back quite a bit! Here's a little something from me to contribute." There's no way the fuzz-covered quarters can even begin to make a dent in the cost of the gift. No, we cannot repay God for what He has done for us.

Even our obedience to God and sacrificial service to Him is ordained, enabled, and empowered by Him. Everything—yes, everything—is from Jesus, through Jesus, and to Jesus. "To Him be glory forever. Amen" (Rom. 11:36). Of course, we don't need PhDs in order to say, "To Jesus be glory forever!" Little children can glorify Christ by their faith in Him.

Can you think of a recent proclamation of Christ's excellencies that came "from the mouths of babes"?

I'm sure we could think of many more precious examples of how little ones praise our Father!

It serves and strengthens our faith when we learn of more reasons why Jesus is the source and goal and glory of our missional motherhood. We'll scratch the surface of another one of those reasons in today's personal study. To do that, let's go to Romans.

In Romans 1, we read a horrific description of what it looks like for image bearers to be entrenched in idolatry. And such were all of us before we came to Christ!

READ ROMANS 1:18-28. To whom is Paul referring? What is the nature of their sinful activity? (Hint: Look at verse 25.)

What happens to them as a result of their idolatry?

Dead in our sin, we are unfit to serve the Creator. Instead, we approve of the idolatry that we and others practice. Not only do we approve it, we applaud it (Rom. 1:32). Then, in His just judgment, God gives us over to our debased minds.

We might say that the first part of Romans (chapters 1–11) describes the gospel, and the rest of the letter (chapters 12–16) spells out the implications (i.e., how we are to live in light of such wonderful truth). Throughout the letter, Paul gives commands to believers because he knows they are alive in Christ, and are therefore able to obey and please God from the heart. They are not obligated to practice idolatry any more because they are now governed by the Holy Spirit and not their flesh. This argument is developed and illustrated throughout the New Testament, but we can see the logic presented rather concisely here in Romans.

> **READ ROMANS 6:10-13.** *Underline all of the phrases that refer to death and life.*

What has Christ died to? Who is Christ alive to? (See v. 10.)

Because we are placed "in Christ" when we are born again, what is the logical connection Paul makes in verse 11?

What are the two corresponding commands to this logical conclusion (vv. 12-13)?

What do you think it means to "present yourselves to God as those who have been brought from death to life"?

What does that look like as a individual follower of Christ? How does that change the way you live your everyday life?

What does that look like as a church? How does that change the way you interact in the body of Christ and present a witness to the world?

This "present yourselves" command shows up again in Romans. We've briefly mentioned Romans 12:1-2 already in this study. Let's ask a few more questions of this passage.

READ ROMANS 12:1-2. What does Paul appeal to his readers to do in verse 1?

According to the passage, how are we to do this?

When the priests in the Old Testament presented the bodies of animals for sacrifice, they slaughtered them. When Jesus, our great High Priest, presented His own body on the cross to be slaughtered as the sacrifice for our sins, this act became to us "the mercy of God." Now, in light of Christ's sacrifice, Paul is appealing to us to make our lives in the body a living sacrifice.

What we are commanded to do in Romans 12:1-2 is the opposite of the idol worship that we read about in Romans 1. When we were dead in our sin we presented our bodies to serve and worship idols. But now, alive in Christ, we present our bodies as living sacrifices to God. The gospel is the means by which our creature-worship is transformed into worship of the one, true God—the Creator.

According to Romans 12:1, what is God's appraisal of our living sacrifices?

Why does God deem our worship—worship from a sinful people—acceptable? How does Hebrews 9:18-22 answer this question?

We have been forgiven, purified, and made acceptable through the blood of Christ. Nothing about us merits acceptance by God. We are welcomed only through the finished work of Christ on the cross. So the ministry that we do while we are still in our physical bodies is done by virtue of the gospel—which is the demonstration of God's profound mercy. It is only because of the gospel of Jesus Christ that we are promised an eternal impact through our missional mothering. Since our new creation life is worship, then all of our ministry is holy and acceptable worship through Christ—from the tiniest cup of water given in Jesus' name to the ultimate sacrifice of giving over our body to persecution unto death.

READ HEBREWS 13:12-16. Meditate on the profound generosity and joy of Jesus. Consider the invitation He gives through His Word in this passage. Journal your reflections below.

There is an epic dedication at the end of Hebrews. It is worth memorizing and reciting in the mornings as you face a long day of ministering to others. Notice the specific character and works of the God who has this exceptional ability to equip us with everything good that we may do His will.

> Now may the God of peace who brought again from the dead our Lord Jesus, the great shepherd of the sheep, by the blood of the eternal covenant, equip you with everything good that you may do his will, working in us that which is pleasing in his sight, through Jesus Christ, to whom be glory forever and ever. Amen.
>
> HEBREWS 13:20-21

Jesus did not simply come to earth to show us how to live the good life so that we could have a fresh start. He came to live and die and live again in our place. Praise Jesus for shedding His blood to secure the eternal covenant that can never be broken. And praise God for raising Him from the dead to be our great Shepherd forever. To Jesus be glory forever and ever, indeed!

It's really great news that God will equip us with everything good that we may do His will.

What are you facing today that you need His equipping for?

FOUR

At some point in your child-rearing and disciple-making, you tell the younger person whom you are teaching, "I can't do this for you. You have to do it yourself." For example, today I told one of my sons that because he is a big boy, there are chores that he has to do himself. A friend and I were talking about how she needed to confess something to her husband. This is also something only she can do. However, at no point do we tell ourselves or anyone else that they must save themselves. Salvation is the work of Jesus Christ. We have done nothing, and we can do nothing to save ourselves. The penalty for sin that Adam and all humanity could never pay, Jesus Himself has paid. The commission in Genesis 1:28, which Adam and all humanity have failed to do, the resurrected and enthroned Jesus is doing through His body here on earth. Isn't it a brilliant wonder, then, that in the opening line of the Book of Acts, Luke says that what he wrote in his Gospel, was "all that Jesus *began* to do and teach" (Acts 1:1, emphasis mine). Through us, now, Jesus is yet working and teaching—He is being fruitful and multiplying His followers across the globe—filling the earth with His glory.

We've examined this passage before, but since it is part of the foundation for missional motherhood, let's look up Genesis 1:28 one more time. What did God tell Adam as the representative head of all humanity, to do?

Describe how Jesus is fulfilling this commission today.

Our missional motherhood is the work of Jesus Christ. Everything we do—from carrying the bodies of our children in our own bodies, to adopting orphans into our families, to praying for least-reached people, to teaching the Bible, to binding up someone's wounds with words of grace or a physical bandage, to giving a cup of cold water in Jesus' name—is done in His name and through His power. Sisters, we are fragile, weak, and helpless creatures. And God has given us "jars of clay" His priceless treasure of the gospel. Why?

> *LOOK UP 2 CORINTHIANS 4:7. Why does God put His treasure in jars of clay like us?*

Later in 2 Corinthians 4, we read some upside-down logic about life and death. This is not your typical "feel good about yourself, Mama!" motivational blog post. You have probably never received a Mother's Day card with this inscription on it. When talk show hosts ask an author to describe to her fans the premise of her new favorite books, the author doesn't say anything remotely close to this. The only place you will find this description of life is in God's Word. Here is what we are doing in our missional motherhood each and every day and night:

> *For we who live are always being given over to death for Jesus' sake, so that the life of Jesus also may be manifested in our mortal flesh.*

2 CORINTHIANS 4:11

Paul is not describing a ministry of empowerment in which we "rise above" worldly obstacles, but one in which we demonstrate that we have passed from death into resurrection life. "The life of Jesus" he is referring to is the indestructible new creation life that Christ now possesses because God raised Him from the dead. Being alive, yet "always being given over to death" is the dynamic at play in our mothering ministries. You have given your life in totality in order to nurture someone else's, but this dying to self for Jesus' sake is what you do a thousand times a day. In those thousands of deaths to self, the life of Jesus—new creation, resurrection life—is shown through you.

Your everyday ministry of motherhood is like an album of living, breathing testimonies of the subversive crucifixion power of Christ. Think of it—Jesus conquered death, sin, and Satan by submitting to death on a cross. All our nurturing work is Jesus working in us and through us to bring glory to Himself. Is it any wonder, then, that all our nurturing work is a death to self? It's all been part of His plan from eternity past. "In his hand is the life of every living thing and the breath of all mankind" (Job 12:10). It is Jesus who is working through you, sister—to Him alone be the glory! He saved us through His gospel, and He has given us His gospel as our reason for living until He takes us home to be with Him forever.

That means we don't have to be afraid to throw ourselves into the good work He has prepared for us (Eph. 2:10), no matter how daunting it seems. It is the indestructible, new creation life of Christ that is at work!

I remember when it became apparent that the surgeries my husband underwent to fix the nerve disorder in his arms did not work. I wept and told God that I could not possibly do what He was calling me to do: be the sole, physical caretaker for our young children and my disabled husband. Obviously, I was looking to "the things that are seen."

How would you encourage a woman who cannot see that the life of Christ is displayed in her deaths-to-self?

Do you need that encouragement today? Explain.

We have the assurance of Christ's unshakable promise that He will be with us even to the end of the age (Matt. 28:18-20). What are some other promises from God's Word that encourage you to persevere by faith?

SESSION 5:
THE KING'S NEW CREATION

REVIEW

Welcome to Session 5 of *Missional Motherhood*! Let's begin by reviewing your homework from last week.

What encouragement does the world offer to women who feel like their work is pointless? How does it ultimately fall short?

Describe the differences between coming to Mount Sinai and to Mount Zion. How can we make it clear to our children and our neighbors that only Christ can fulfill all the law's demands? How can we demonstrate to others that our hope is in Christ alone?

How is Jesus currently fulfilling the commission in Genesis 1:28?

How would you encourage a woman who can't see that the life of Christ is displayed in her deaths-to-self?

Does anyone in the room need to hear those words of encouragement today?

What favorite Scripture passages encourage you to hold on to Christ by faith as you go about the good work He has prepared for you?

WATCH

Use the space below to take notes on the Session 5 video.

DISCUSS

Use the following questions to debrief the teaching from the Session 5 video.

Sometimes when you share God's truth with someone who is spiritually blind and deaf, you are met with hostility. What encourages you when this happens?

Why is it so hard to "forget the former things" (i.e., the world that is passing away), and focus on the new creation that God is creating?

What did Jesus tell the Samaritan woman about Himself in John 4? Who are the "Samaritans" in your community and where do they gather? How can you be a part of witnessing to them about where they can find living water?

We're coming full circle back to the "just a mom" issue. How has your perspective changed on this over the past weeks?

"Evangelism is mom's work, but the giving of faith is God's." How else could you restate that truth?

CLOSE

Lead in prayer for the women who said they need encouragement to see a display of the life of Christ in their deaths-to-self. Perhaps you could pray through some of the favorite Scripture passages your group mentioned.

ONE

In our discussion of missional mothering, we need to talk about homemaking. There, I said it. (Were you waiting for me to say it?) I wonder what kind of things just leaped into your mind. Now would be a good time to say those things, so here are a few starter questions for discussion:

What comes to mind when you think about homemaking?

What might be the connection between our homemaking and our missional mothering?

The classic text for Christian women to discuss when they talk about homemaking is Titus 2. And no wonder! This passage connects dots between the gospel, woman-to-woman discipleship, marriage, motherhood, local church, and the home. We don't have time to dive deep into every one of these things this week, so we'll just be focusing on the home.

Most of us wake up every day in our own homes. The home, as we see in Titus 2, is actually not an accessory to display our unique personalities (contrary to popular Western opinions). Homemaking is a strategic everyday ministry designed by God to adorn His gospel in this age where the new creation has broken into the old age. Phew! That's a big sentence. I hope the work we are about to do in studying the passage will unpack that thought. It's important that we understand the statement because our homemaking, when carried out in light of the cosmic ramifications of the resurrection of Jesus, is a ministry that can shake the gates of hell.

Knowing the context of Scripture is important, so here is a little background on Paul's Letter to Titus, pastor of the church at Crete. Though the letter was written nearly two thousand years ago, it has a contemporary feel to it.

Cities across the globe tend to have a "vibe" to them—something they are known for. All I have to do is say the word *Paris* and you quickly think of sights, sounds and even feelings that are associated with the City of Light. Then there's Los Angeles, Rio de Janeiro, Delhi, and so many others. The reputations of these cities are known to us whether or not we have been a citizen or a visitor.

Back in Paul's day, Rome was purported to be the eternal city. It was the happening place. The borders of Rome were ever-expanding, and it was the capital city of everything powerful, wealthy, and glorious. Rome was where history was headed, and if you were against her… well, then, you were on "the wrong side of history." To her citizens Rome symbolized hope, peace, and prosperity.

What does this description of Rome call to mind?

Crete had been subsumed into the Roman Empire only a few generations prior to Paul's letter. What kind of struggles would these Cretan Christians have faced because of Rome's influence in their society?

READ TITUS 1:10-16. What were the issues facing the Cretan church?

What was the result of the hypocrisy that Paul pointed out in verse 16?

Paul had better things in mind regarding the Cretan believers, who had been saved out of this mess of depraved humanity. Jesus had ransomed them from their former ways by His own blood, and made them to be part of His new creation. Their life "in Christ" was the basis for Pastor Titus's ministry to them. Paul left Titus behind in Crete to rebuke the false teachers, teach truth to the new believers, and raise up elders to lead them. These young Christians needed to grow up through Titus's teaching "what accords with sound doctrine" (Titus 2:1).

Paul's instructions that followed dealt with their expressions of authenticity as new creations. The Cretan believers had undergone a night-and-day transformation. Their dead souls had been raised to life. When we study what Paul taught and consider the application for our lives, we must remember that it is "what accords with sound doctrine." That doctrine is the gospel—the Word of Christ. It's the will of God. These doctrinally grounded commands are for God's glory and our good from the One who created us, knows what's best for us, and knows how He will be best magnified in His image bearers.

> *Most of us appreciate and find useful a list of practical helps. We can all benefit from the wisdom of "5 Steps to_____," or "3 Keys to _____." However, we need to be careful to teach the sound doctrine that is foundational for the practical "to dos." What can be the consequences of only checking off the "to dos" and forgetting the "whys" behind them?*

> *Name one or two different ministries that you lead or participate in on a regular basis. How are you encouraged when you remember the "why" of why you do them?*

Paul wrote that this life is temporary and fleeting, and that we were saved in hope of eternal life. We are coheirs together. As easy as it is to get sucked back in to the course of this world or discouraged by the mundane of every day life, we need to keep our focus on things that are unseen. We need to keep this eternal view as we study Titus 2. It seems on the surface as though Paul is exhorting women to only concern themselves with things that are seen, such as husbands, children, and homes. But we need to remember that there is something unseen and spiritually powerful going on as we prioritize those ministries. It's resurrection life.

So, here's what it looks like for the Cretan church (and you and me) to be pleasing to the Lord, obedient, and fit for every good work:

READ TITUS 2:1-15 THREE TIMES THROUGH. *What words stand out to you in Paul's description of the Christian life in a post-Easter world?*

We'll examine this text more closely in the next personal study session.

TWO

We know that Easter changed everything. When Jesus died and was resurrected, He inaugurated a new age that fractured the old one, so that the present form of this world is now passing away (1 Cor. 7:31). This is the reality Paul was writing about. We live in a post-Easter world, managing little gospel outposts for spreading the good news. The sovereign Lord Jesus is ascended, exalted, and reigning. His kingdom is coming, and it is the antitype of the City of Man and all the mini-City of Man wannabes like Rome.

Let's see how this reality is illustrated in Paul's instructions in Titus 2. Remember, Paul was writing to a pastor (Titus), telling him how discipleship ought to work in the church at Crete. Paul wants Pastor Titus to "teach what accords with sound doctrine" (Titus 2:1). The "sound doctrine" is the gospel of Jesus Christ. So, the instructions that follow are exactly that: what accords with the gospel.

READ TITUS 2:1-15. Now, zoom in on verses 3-5. What is the teaching that accords with sound doctrine—the gospel?

Who is to be doing the teaching in these verses?

What is the reason given in verse 5?

Look up the word revile in the dictionary. Copy the definition below.

Let's talk more about the word *revile*. I don't know about you, but I don't typically use that word in my everyday vocabulary.

The Greek word is *blasphemetai*, from where we get our word *blasphemy*. It's possible that the teachings about Christian freedom emanating from the gospel had led to some confusion or compromise about the God-given order in the home. This was leading some of the Jewish false teachers to bring charges of blasphemy against the gospel message or caused them to revile the Word of God. Paul urged Titus to make clear God's instructions for the home according to the Scriptures.[1]

Paul spoke to a similar issue In 1 Timothy 5:3-14. In this passage, Paul gave instruction on how the church ought to take care of widows, and which widows the church ought to take care of. In the course of his instructions he mentioned younger widows and warned that they were vulnerable to becoming "idlers, going about from house to house, and not only idlers, but also gossips and busybodies, saying what they should not" (v. 13). So Paul's instruction was clear, "I would have younger widows marry, bear children, manage their households, and give the adversary no occasion for slander" (v. 14). Paul's exhortation to Pastor Timothy was that he counsel the younger widows to marry again, raise families, and manage their homes because Satan was ready and willing to give them a different calling.

What is the connection between believers living rightly in light of the gospel, and the enemies of God slandering the gospel?

What is the opposite of reviling the word of God, or slandering the gospel?

READ TITUS 2:1-10. What is the "so that" reason given for this new code of conduct (v. 8)?

In our everyday mothering ministry, Christ's lordship over the world and His ongoing activity in the world come to light. Jesus said in Acts 1:8 that we will be His witnesses from Judea, to Samaria, to the outermost parts of the earth. This witnessing is happening when we open our mouths to intentionally convey the gospel message to a nonbeliever. We adorn the truth to which we are witnessing by what we do and refrain from doing. When older women teach younger women to love their husbands and children and manage their homes with Christ's lordship in view, they are acting in line with the reality of the new creation in Christ. When we live contradictory to the truth, we live as though we are still dead in our sins, and we leave the gospel open to be slandered or reviled. However, when our actions line up with God's Word, we bear a clear gospel witness, and His truth is beautifully adorned.

1. Thomas Lea and Hayne P. Griffin, *1, 2 Timothy, Titus*, vol. 34 in New American Commentary (Nashville: Broadman Press, 1992).

THREE

For my kindergarten-aged son, life revolves around Wednesdays. Wednesday is his turn to bring a toy to school for "Show and Tell." He's naturally a little shy, but on Wednesdays, he has an opportunity to stand up in front of the class, show them one of his beloved toys, and answer questions from the other kids. "Show and Tell" is his big chance to say what's on his heart—he's the one holding the object of discussion, he is the "expert" on that toy, and the floor is his. As believers in Christ, we have a Show and Tell ministry as we live out our faith in this lost world. Our works adorn the gospel words we speak, showing others what this message of hope in Christ looks like in practical ways.

The "good works" theme comes up a lot in Paul's Letter to Titus. The term occurs 13 times in the New Testament, and one third of those instances are in Titus. What do the following verses in Titus say about our good works?

Titus 2:7

Titus 2:14

Titus 3:8

Titus 3:14

If we are saved by grace through faith, why are good works such a big deal? The potential for God's Word to be reviled is great if we don't make our words and actions line up with the gospel we profess. Our "Show and Tell" needs to match up, otherwise we have an integrity problem.

> *READ DEUTERONOMY 4:5-8. Moses was explaining to the nation of Israel the attractional nature of their status as God's people and their relationship to God's law. What were the Israelites to do?*

> *What would be the benefit to them of doing so?*

> *According to the passage, how would the nations respond?*

We certainly want our own lives to be an occasion for the nations to say, "What god is like their God?" So, how can we become fit for every good work? We should adorn the doctrine of God by consuming, loving, obeying, and teaching the Word of God.

> *READ 2 TIMOTHY 3:16-17. What does God's Word do for us? What is the outcome?*

> *Since Scripture does all of this for us, through us, and in us, how can we demonstrate its importance in our lives?*

It's funny and frustrating to think that we can use the best homemaking techniques to clean our homes, but before long the house is dirty again. (I have four kids—I know!). But the Word of God that does the work of God in our hearts leads to spiritual fruit that lasts into eternity.

God's Word accomplishes God's will in our lives. We submit to Him, embrace His will as our own, and behold the beauty of His Son as we gaze into the Scriptures day after day. Now, lest we feel discouraged by the hard-core, radical, new creation imperatives we've just read in this chapter in Titus, we need to remember the hope of the gospel. God is the One working to accomplish these things in us and through us. Just look at the next verse in Titus 2.

> *READ TITUS 2:11-14. Because of Jesus' comprehensive work on the cross, "the grace of God has appeared." What is God's grace to us through Jesus accomplishing?*

> *What is our "blessed hope?"*

> *Why did Jesus give Himself for us?*

> *Who are the "people for his own possession"?*

> *How can you help your sisters in Christ look to our shared blessed hope?*

Do you see that this structure for discipleship and the woman's home-oriented ministry is not about efficiency or cultural ideal? Can you see the focus of our missional motherhood zoom in and out with cosmic, grand implications because of Christ's death and resurrection? Jesus Christ is the greatest missional home manager the world has ever seen. He builds His house and He sets His house in order. He is head over His church and He loves her perfectly. He nourishes her with His Word. Christ reigns in sovereign superiority; He is the basis of all our joy. We must live our lives focused on His sovereign lordship over the cosmos.

We bear fruit of His Spirit, living self-controlled, upright, and godly lives now as we wait for His appearing. He is our blessed hope.

So, does bringing our home under the lordship of Christ and waiting for His return mean that our house must be pristine clean all the time? I don't think so, and I sure hope not. I moved aside a pile of unfolded laundry so I could sit in this chair to type. Is the question that Titus 2 answers, "Can women hold jobs outside their homes?" There are some who think so, but that is missing the forest for the trees. The question that Titus answers is this: "How can we as Christian women work in such a way that the holiness and hope of God is evident in our lives?" Titus 2 is not about how Christian women need to be domestic goddesses; it's about how Christian women point people to God through their homes. That is what accords with sound doctrine—the gospel. Faithfulness in the practical matters of loving our husband and children and managing our homes honors the gospel and shows the world the beauty of the gospel. We don't manage our homes because our homes are our hope. We manage our homes because Christ is our hope.

> Take a moment to consider and answer this question: How can we as Christian women work in such a way that the holiness and hope of God is evident in our lives?

> How does this relate to your participation in your local church?

FOUR

Use this last personal study as a review of all you've heard and studied over the last several weeks. Here are some reflection questions to prompt your review:

What was your view of motherhood before you started this study? Did you view it as part of the eternal plan of God to increase His kingdom? Why or why not?

List below four to six key things the Lord has taught you in His Word through this study.

List some mothers you know who need to be encouraged in their ministry of motherhood. How can you encourage them?

How has your heart been encouraged by what Jesus has done and is doing in redeeming a people for Himself?

How has your view of motherhood changed through this study?

How will life be different for you in the days to come as a result of what God has taught you through Missional Motherhood?

SESSION 6:

MISSIONAL MOTHERHOOD REACHES FROM THE HOME TO THE WORLD

REVIEW

Welcome to Session 6 of *Missional Motherhood*! Let's begin by reviewing your homework from last week.

What comes to mind when you think about homemaking?

Discuss this statement: "Homemaking is a strategic everyday ministry designed by God to adorn His gospel in this age where the new creation has broken in to the old age."

We can all benefit from the wisdom of "5 Steps to _____" or "3 Keys to _____." However, we need to be careful to teach the sound doctrine that is foundational for the practical "to dos." What is this sound doctrine? And what is the result of only checking off the "to dos" and forgetting the "whys" behind them?

We live in a post-Easter world managing little gospel outposts for spreading the good news. What are some of the ways in which your home is "a little gospel outpost"?

Our works adorn the gospel words we speak, showing others what this message of hope in Christ looks like in practical ways. What are some examples of this happening in your everyday mothering ministry?

Discuss this statement: "We don't manage our homes because our homes are our hope. We manage our homes because Christ is our hope."

WATCH

Use the space below to take notes on the Session 6 video.

DISCUSS

Use the following questions to debrief the teaching from the Session 6 video.

Discuss this statement: "God's Word helps remind us that missional motherhood is a strategic tool in the nail-scarred hands of the One who is summing up all things in Himself."

Here are the three "already/even now" statements. Which one do you find the greatest challenge to believe?

- *God has made you a citizen of heaven, even now making you a pilgrim who is on her way to the city whose builder and architect is God.*

- *God has powerfully and irrevocably resurrected you, even now making you a participant and part of His permanent new creation in this world that is passing away.*

- *God has given His Spirit to dwell in you, even now making you a living stone in His temple, the dwelling place of God among men.*

This is a controversial statement in many subcultures: "In Titus 2 we saw how we're free to throw ourselves into the noble, Great Commission work of training up younger women and prioritizing the ministry in our homes." How would this perspective reshape your faith community?

The quote in the video from DeYoung and Gilbert's book, What is the Mission of the Church?, *could also raise eyebrows in some places. Recalling what you've learned in this study, what is God's mission? What is the church's mission? What is your mission?*

What is the assurance we have that God's mission will be accomplished? How does this assurance encourage and strengthen your heart today?

CLOSE

Provide time for the ladies to share insights from the last personal study session. Discuss together how God has changed and shaped you all during this study.

Lead each person in your group to choose a partner. Direct the pairs to pray for one another as they go and mother disciples to God's glory. Encourage the ladies to exchange contact details with one another so they can follow up with each other and continue to build relationships of mutual support in their missional motherhood.

NOTES

NOTES

NOTES

WE LOVE NEW FRIENDS!

Stop by the LifeWay Women blog.

lifewaywomen.com

Sign up for our weekly newsletter at lifeway.com/WomensNews

THERE IS NO SUCH THING AS "JUST"
A MOM IN THE GRAND PLAN OF GOD.

Follow Gloria Furman in the book that inspired the study
as she traces God's mission for motherhood throughout
the entire Bible—showing how this mission impacts the
everyday ministry of all women.

:: CROSSWAY | CROSSWAY.ORG